*Building Effective Nonprofit Boards*

**BoardSource**, formerly the National Center for Nonprofit Boards, is the premier resource for practical information, tools and best practices, training, and leadership development for board members of nonprofit organizations worldwide. Through our highly acclaimed programs and services, BoardSource enables organizations to fulfill their missions by helping build strong and effective nonprofit boards.

BoardSource provides

- Resources to nonprofit leaders through our workshops, training, and our extensive Web site, www.boardsource.org

- Governance consultants who work directly with nonprofit leaders to design specialized solutions to meet an organization's needs

- Tools on nonprofit governance, including more than 100 booklets, books, videos, CDs, and audiotapes

- An annual conference that brings together approximately 800 board members and chief executives of nonprofit organizations from around the world

For more information, please visit our Web site at www.boardsource.org, e-mail us at mail@boardsource.org, or call us at 800-883-6262.

# Contents

## *Introduction*
# TO GO FORWARD, RETREAT!

In most contexts, the word *retreat* suggests the act of running away from a difficult situation. But for nonprofit board members who have participated in successful retreats, the term has exactly the opposite connotation. A well-planned, inclusively conceived, effectively executed retreat is perhaps the best way to address head-on some of the more challenging issues facing a board and the organization it governs. Because a board retreat is an unparalleled opportunity for progress, perhaps a better term for the kind of focused, action-oriented meeting that is advocated in these pages would be *forward retreat*, or *strategic meeting*.

Like anything worth doing, a *forward retreat* doesn't just happen. It requires careful planning and a significant commitment of resources, time, and creative energy — by planners, by the organization's staff, and by participants. The *forward retreat* approach can rarely be accomplished within the quintessential retreat format in which planners don't consult members in setting meeting objectives, the schedule is often inflexible, and activities are usually generic.

Participants in such retreats recognize that their input is not really desired and find that the meeting's results have little impact on the real work of the organization or board. Unfortunately, nonprofit board members who have endured poorly planned or implemented retreats may come to expect that all retreats are at best exercises in futility and at worst a waste of time and resources.

Recently, retreat planning has been injected with fresh energy and creativity. Organizers do their best to engage and keep the attention of participants with hands-on activities, team-building games, small-group discussions, and opportunities for exploration. A *forward retreat* goes one step further — tying the meeting's agenda and activities clearly to the organization's strategic challenges and goals.

Boards that regularly engage in *forward retreats* know that the time spent away from the press of daily responsibilities and tasks can allow the board to challenge assumptions and rethink systems, begin a strategic planning process, tackle

> *A retreat seems the right place to help the board refocus its activities.... Board meetings are pretty formal days. It's hard to relax and engage in the honest and open conversations needed to build an understanding of the dreams that we all share for this organization.*
>
> — John Roberts,
> Chair, Board of Trustees
> Epworth Children's Home
> Columbia, South Carolina

> *One of the biggest advantages for our board in holding a retreat is the better understanding they gain of where the Association is headed and how we're going to get there. We leave each retreat feeling much less fragmented and more of a board "team" having discussed the common issues that affect us all.*
>
> — Susan Lengal
> Executive Director
> Akron Bar Association
> Akron, Ohio

difficult issues, forge camaraderie, and improve productivity. In fact, the effectiveness of such meetings is causing many boards to reengineer their regular meeting schedules and formats to mirror the qualities of a *forward retreat*, which:

■ **Sets realistic objectives** — allowing time to address a few issues in depth rather than trying to cover too many topics in a short time; setting achievable retreat goals; and using the retreat to develop initiatives and plans that can actually be implemented.

■ **Addresses meaningful topics** — avoiding routine business or trivia that can better be dispatched at regular board meetings, through committees, or by staff.

■ **Engages the participation and input of all board members** — and may even include people from the organization's key internal and external constituencies if they have a stake in the issues being addressed at the retreat.

■ **Tailors activities** to the specific culture and structure of the board and organization.

■ **Is flexible** enough in format to allow time for participants to explore ideas that arise unex-

pectedly during the retreat.

■ **Is enjoyable** for everyone involved, providing plenty of opportunities for participants to socialize and strengthen their relationships with one another.

A successful retreat can hinge on the work of a hard-working planning committee, a skilled facilitator, dynamic speakers, and an executive who carries out preparation down to the last detail. It can be helped along by an agreeable locale and energizing activities. But the most important factor contributing to the success of a retreat is a planning process that involves board members.

This booklet provides strategies and tools to begin the process of planning a *forward retreat*. If there is one rule of retreat planning, it's that there are no hard-and-fast rules. Every organization is different — and no organization stays the same from year to year. So instead of providing you with "model retreat agendas" that can be applied to any organization, we offer a retreat planning process that can be adapted to your organization's specific needs and resources.

*Section One*
# WHY?

A *forward retreat* works best when it is organized in order to achieve clearly defined objectives — not simply to fill a predetermined amount of time. Because a retreat is a focused, special kind of meeting, it can easily be harnessed to a specific set of tasks. The *why* of a board retreat will usually grow out of a consideration of the unique culture and current circumstances of your organization and board.

Most boards can benefit from an annual retreat even if its goal is the same each year: for example, "to strengthen our relationships with one another and refresh our understanding of the organization's current and future challenges." To get the most out of a retreat, however, a board should go into it with a clearly defined list of objectives, not a general desire to simply improve board effectiveness. After all, clear objectives provide an effective way to measure the retreat's success.

No matter what its specific objectives, a board retreat can yield a broad range of benefits. It can be:

■ an opportunity for planning and team-building that the press of regular board activities simply won't allow;

■ a chance to refocus on fundamentals, to engage in thoughtful strategic planning, to reflect on mission, vision, and strategic goals;

■ a vehicle for strengthening trust and relationships among board members, between board and staff, or for pulling together a divided board on a critical issue; and

■ a time to conduct a self-assessment of the board.

The knowledge, spirit, and common direction that often emerge from an effective board retreat will benefit the board long after the sessions end. So, taking the time up front to engage in thoughtful retreat planning — usually two to four months is sufficient — can yield not only an enjoyable, effective retreat, but also long-term benefits for the board.

## Gaining Leadership Commitment

We've all attended meetings that thinned out in the afternoon as participants, following the lead of senior executives, crept off to check voice mail or attend to "important" tasks back at the office. As in any endeavor, top-level commitment is essential to the success of a board retreat. The board will take its cue from how the board chair, the chief executive, the officers, and more senior, respected board members approach the retreat. The best way to gain leadership commitment is to ensure that the retreat will enhance the effectiveness of the board and the organization and that everyone's ideas and opinions are needed and valued. Top-level commitment is revealed when:

■ The board chair strongly endorses the retreat and becomes involved in the planning process.

■ The chair appoints a retreat planning committee, or specifically charges a standing committee with retreat-preparation responsibility.

■ The retreat is planned far enough in advance so a date can be selected when most board members will be available.

■ The chief executive becomes personally involved in the planning process.

■ The retreat planning committee seeks board members' input through pre-retreat interviews or questionnaires and past retreat evaluations and suggestions.

■ The board allocates a sufficient budget so that the retreat's purposes aren't compromised by inadequate facilities or support.

■ Board members commit the time to prepare for and attend the retreat, recognizing that the retreat is just as important as participation in other board functions.

## Establishing a Retreat Planning Committee

Although the primary responsibility for planning board retreats falls on the board itself, members must rely extensively on the chief executive for assistance on many fronts — from engaging a facilitator to suggesting and contacting speakers to coordinating facility arrangements. The chief executive is thus often both a member of and staff to the committee. The retreat planning committee is generally responsible for making substantive decisions about the retreat, leaving administrative tasks to the executive. The committee's focus should be on:

■ Developing and approving retreat goals.

■ Developing an invitation list.

■ Promoting attendance.

■ Suggesting or approving timing and location.

■ Approving the facilitator and speakers.

■ Commenting on pre-retreat questionnaires and the retreat agenda.

■ Coordinating retreat follow-up.

## Setting Clear and Realistic Goals

A board retreat is a focused, time-limited activity. At best, the board should expect to focus on one or two main issues during the retreat. One of the biggest mistakes that boards make in planning retreats is having overly high expectations. A retreat is not going to solve major problems, although it can be a helpful first step in charting a course through difficult waters.

Setting realistic goals often means leaving implementation planning for a later date. Board members, who usually hold leadership roles in most areas of their lives, should not be expected to work out the details. The board's

strength is often in guiding discussions about vision and mission, and providing oversight. In planning board retreats, keep in mind the unique role of the governing board.

Typical issues addressed at board retreats include:

**1. Strategic planning.** Because a retreat takes the board away from day-to-day tasks, it is an outstanding opportunity to address long-range issues such as:

■ Reviewing and revising the organization's mission statement and vision for the future. This can include considering changes in the organization's structure — such as mergers or strategic alliances.

■ Reviewing recent achievements, assessing organizational and environmental changes, and approving future initiatives.

**2. Education on timely subjects.** As the organization approaches new challenges, it's helpful to take time out to bring the board up to speed on new developments in the organization's field or on topics of particular interest. The board can use an educational retreat to:

■ Explore the impact on the organization of a significant topic, such as fund development, changing demographics, program expansion, or legislative issues and legal challenges. Such a retreat could also be helpful to assess the need for investment in new technological resources. In fact, many boards are using the retreat format to assess their organization's (and their own) technological needs in an era when e-mail, videoconferencing, and distance learning may help an organization better achieve its mission.

■ Take action related to the topic — such as gaining board commitment for a capital campaign or approval of a technology plan.

### 3. Self-assessment and board development.

Boards have long used annual retreats to engage in regular self-assessment and to facilitate the evolution of the board. The role of an impartial facilitator is important in conducting retreats of this type. A regular annual retreat can be a time to provide ongoing leadership training to all board members and mentoring from experienced to newer members. A retreat can also be extremely useful whenever the board is at a point of transition — when senior board leaders are rotating off the board, for example, or when the board has received an infusion of young members and finds itself facing issues of communication and collaboration among different generations. A self-assessment retreat can allow a board to undertake such specific tasks as:

■ Evaluating its roles, responsibilities, relationships, structure, work processes, recruitment mechanism, and overall effec-

tiveness — and identifying opportunities for improvement.

■ Examining the relationships among a national board, regional boards, affiliate organizations' boards, and local chapters.

■ Revising the organization's bylaws and committee structure or rethinking the nature and structure of board meetings to accommodate the working styles and values of board members of different generations — and to accomplish the work of the board in an effective and efficient way.

### 4. Relationship-building.

Any retreat can and should include activities designed to build relationships among board members. A board that is not working effectively may also consider devoting an entire retreat to relationship-building with a skilled facilitator through Outward Bound–style or (depending on the board's style, fitness, and age) less strenuous trust- and team-building activities. Key objectives for such a retreat may include:

■ Identifying barriers to collaboration.

■ Building bridges to improve communication, trust, and cohesiveness.

> *One of the biggest challenges with a retreat is to enter the process with realistic expectations. People think that a retreat is a process for finding solutions. I've found that a retreat is more useful as a tool for identifying issues that are much too big to be resolved over the course of two or three days. The best outcome would be to leave with a list of things to keep working on.*
>
> — Sue Bunting
> Executive Director
> Foundation for Seacoast Health
> Portsmouth, New Hampshire

■ Strengthening the board–chief executive relationship.

■ Improving relations between the board and professional staff (hospital medical staff, foundation staff, or university faculty, for example), or helping the board better understand the concerns of institutional constituencies — clients, volunteers, students, members, grantees, neighbors.

A pre-retreat questionnaire is a useful tool for the retreat planning committee to discover the issues most relevant to the board at this time. Reaching out to all potential retreat participants — and other constituencies as well — helps to ensure that all retreat participants understand that their input is desired and valued. For example, if long-range planning is needed but half of the board isn't speaking to the other half, then devoting retreat time to building relationships may be more effective than diving right into a strategic planning exercise.

The sample pre-retreat questionnaire on page 9 offers a suggestion for organizing this initial information-gathering effort. Of course, the options provided should be specific to your organization's current needs. The agenda options the retreat planning committee offers on the pre-retreat questionnaire can be gathered through brainstorming sessions by the committee, often working closely with a facilitator and sometimes in consultation with members of important constituencies — board members, community leaders, staff, clients.

The key in the *why* phase of retreat planning is to be as inclusive as possible. As Thomas Holland noted in an article about retreat planning, without including every board member in identifying issues to be addressed in the retreat, "a chief executive officer or board chair may be able to persuade a board to go through the motions of a retreat — but not to the degree that it would if the whole board were closely involved in the process from the beginning."

The following questionnaire is designed to help with pre-retreat planning. It can be customized for your organization and faxed, mailed, or e-mailed to all board members (and possibly other key constituents) at the beginning of the retreat planning process. The questionnaire can come from the board chair, the retreat planning chair, or both, with a joint letter.

# Pre-Retreat Planning Questionnaire — Part 1

**Organization:** _____

**Date of retreat:** _____

**Location of retreat:** _____

In order to prepare the most effective agenda for our upcoming retreat, we need to hear from you. Please complete and return this form to us by _____. Please tell us:

**1. What are the 3-5 major issues facing our *organization* in the next five years?**

_____

_____

_____

_____

**2. What are the 3-5 major issues facing the *board* in the next five years?**

_____

_____

_____

_____

**3. What are some suggestions for ways that we can better serve our clients/ members/grantees?**

_____

_____

_____

_____

# Pre-Retreat Planning Questionnaire — Part 2

*[Faxed, mailed, or e-mailed to all retreat participants once key issues have been identified and the agenda is being drafted.]*

**1. Please rank the following proposed goals for this year's retreat in order of importance (1 being most important for the board to achieve at this time):**

- ❏ To understand the challenges facing our organization in today's environment.
- ❏ To discuss strategic directions our organization should take in the future.
- ❏ To evaluate the board's performance and identify areas for improvement.
- ❏ To discuss the relationship between the board and executive staff, and how the relationship could be improved.
- ❏ Other:

**2. Please rank the following proposed retreat topics in order of importance (1 being most important to address at this time):**

- ❏ Board/management roles, relationships, and communications.
- ❏ The board's role in fund-raising.
- ❏ The structure and frequency of board meetings.
- ❏ The organization's progress in achieving goals from our last strategic plan.
- ❏ A clearer sense of the organization's programs.
- ❏ Community relations issues facing the organization and board.
- ❏ Recent changes in environment in which our organization exists.
- ❏ Changing needs of our traditional constituents.
- ❏ Issues relating to our tax-exempt status.
- ❏ Other:

**3. Of the proposed topics listed under #2 above, which *two*, in your opinion, should receive the greatest emphasis at the retreat?**

a)

b)

**4. Should the retreat include outside speakers? If yes, who do you believe would be appropriate speakers for the retreat?**

**5. Please rank the following proposed locations (1 being the location you would prefer the most, 2 being your second choice, etc.).**

❑ Grand Hotel Downtown (theater/opera package)
❑ Golf Club (golf, tennis)
❑ University Conference Center (golf, tennis)
❑ Lodge at State Park (nature walks, canoeing)
❑ Other:

**6. Please rank the following proposed times (1 being the most convenient for you; 3 being the least convenient):**

❑ Friday Night/Saturday
❑ Saturday/Sunday
❑ Weekdays with overnight; best day(s):

**7. Other suggestions for this year's retreat:**

## Section Two
# WHO?

Who should attend a board retreat? The answer to that question depends largely on the retreat's goals and content. Clearly, if the board will be addressing sensitive or confidential issues, then participation should be limited to the board, and no outsiders should be present at meetings. However, if the purpose of the retreat is to deliberate on the future of the organization, to decide on whether a merger or even dissolution of the organization's charter is needed, then it may be appropriate to include key constituents in discussions.

Multiconstituency retreats bring together people with a wide range of relationships to the organization and can often offer the board a fresh look at issues important to its organization's strength and even survival, or it may take the form of a carefully planned and led "Futures Conference."

## Selecting a Facilitator

Every retreat needs a facilitator — someone who can help the board plan and conduct the retreats. A facilitator should not be expected to participate in this retreat as a working "attendee," nor should the facilitator have any stake in the proceedings except to ensure that the participants are fully engaged in activities and that the board accomplishes its retreat objectives. A good facilitator can:

- Assist with retreat planning, drafting pre-retreat questionnaires, and conducting pre-retreat interviews and discussions.

- Suggest locations, speakers, and retreat activities to support objectives.

- Inject objectivity and experience into retreat planning, data-gathering, and meeting discussions.

- Allow the board chair to participate freely, without the responsibility of conducting the meeting.

- Keep the discussion focused and moving, and stimulate participation without allowing any one person or group to dominate.

- Engage participants in group-process and team-building activities.

- Play devil's advocate, encouraging the board to discuss uncomfortable but important issues.

- Play peacemaker and keep conflict from turning destructive.

- Drive the retreat toward closure.

- Prepare a post-retreat summary.

- Assist the board after the retreat to implement recommendations or plan future retreats.

The two essential requirements for an effective retreat facilitator are objectivity and expertise. Most often, the first of these characteristics can best be found in an outsider. However, it can be a challenge to find an outsider who really understands your organization's culture, language, pace, and style. A facilitator not only has to be neutral during the retreat, but also must understand how participants think, make decisions, and handle conflict in order to help them achieve consensus.

The best way to find an outside facilitator is to request recommendations from other organizations similar to yours. A facilitator who works most often with attorneys may not understand the different pace and values of an arts organization's board or the board of an organization serving the homeless. Other sources of referrals to facilitators include local Support Centers, Councils on Agencies, listservs, and Internet searches. Don't fall into the trap of using the same facilitator every year. Facilitators who are too familiar with your group can lose their objectivity and may lack the ability to bring in a fresh perspective.

Before engaging a facilitator, the retreat planning committee may wish to interview two or three consultants. Always check professional references before engaging any consultant, and before the facilitator begins working with your retreat planning committee, make sure you have in hand a signed letter of agreement outlining the specific terms of the engagement, the exact services the facilitator will provide, fees and expenses, and a signed confidentiality agreement, if appropriate. Even if your facilitator is offering pro bono services, it's important to spell out exactly what is expected.

Involve the facilitator as early as possible in the retreat planning process, and provide him or her with background information on the organization (bylaws, strategic plan, mission statement, latest audited financial statement, and other key documents). If appropriate, the facilitator may also find it helpful to review a copy of the minutes from the last meeting. Spend some time talking about the board culture and internal politics. There should be no surprises for the facilitator. If the chief executive is in danger of losing his or her job, or should there be an unresolved issue that is brought up at every meeting, the facilitator should know about any potential problems before attending the retreat. With a clear picture of the institution, the facilitator can steer clear of land mines or anticipate ways of handling certain situations.

If you choose *not* to engage a facilitator — although we strongly suggest that you do — then someone from inside the organization will need to run the retreat. Often, this task will fall to the board chair. A disadvantage of this approach is that having the usual authority figure run the meeting could inhibit discussion or allow the retreat to fall into the pattern of regular board meetings.

Even more important, a facilitator cannot both run the meeting and participate fully. So if the board chair wants to be actively involved in shaping the new mission or contributing to board self-assessment, someone else should serve as facilitator.

> *We are currently going through some major changes and growing pains and are suddenly faced with conflicts about the organization's direction.... In these situations, it is very helpful to have an outside moderator who can ask the hard questions that colleagues wouldn't ordinarily ask one another.*
>
> — Sue Bunting
> Executive Director
> Foundation for
> Seacoast Health
> Portsmouth, New
> Hampshire

## Developing the Invitation List

A board will often choose to invite other organization constituents — staff, clients, members, grantees, volunteers, neighbors, community leaders — to participate in all or part of a board retreat. The decision to include others in the board retreat should be made after a careful consideration of retreat goals. Others who may be invited to participate in a board retreat include:

■ **The chief executive.** Even though the organization's chief executive is usually not a board member, he or she is normally invited to board retreats. The executive is the board's leader-in-residence, and it is difficult to imagine a retreat without him or her. The chief executive may be excused if executive assessment is on the retreat agenda. The chief executive is often the only staff member present at board self-assessment retreats.

■ **Other senior managers and professional staff.** Everyone whose input is essential to further the discussion and enhance the retreat objectives should be invited to a retreat. For example, staff frequently participate in strategic planning retreats. Some boards, as a sign of mutual trust, may also invite the management team to participate in an examination of the governance process and board-management relationships. In deciding whether to invite management to attend a board retreat, the retreat planning committee should clearly outline what role staff participants will play — will they participate fully, serve only as an information resource, attend social functions, facilitate group discussions, or simply observe?

■ **Other constituencies.** When the retreat agenda includes items that will affect a variety of constituencies — friends, donors, neighbors, members, community leaders, volunteers, grantees, clients — it may be appropriate to solicit the input of these constituents as a part of the retreat process. For example, boards using a retreat to consider a merger or a major shift in programmatic offerings may want to include representatives of groups that will be affected by the change. Including leaders from outside the board structure in a board retreat can also help boards that are working to increase their own diversity to identify potential candidates for board service.

■ **Spouses and guests.** The decision to invite spouses sometimes can be a source of controversy in the retreat-planning process. Some

> *In multiconstituent retreats, or retreats where spouses and family members are in attendance, everyone needs to know what sessions they are invited to attend and what role they can play. Can they participate in discussions, add agenda items, vote? All of this must be spelled out in advance.*
>
> — Bill Dietel
> Chair,
> Pierson-Lovelace
> Foundation
> Los Angeles, California

board members may object to the additional costs or distraction from business. Boards of public agencies are especially sensitive to criticism of "junkets" at taxpayer expense. But there are good reasons to invite spouses. If the retreat goals and objectives involve relationship-building, the presence of spouses can set a more informal tone. Board members may be more willing to participate in longer retreats (two to three days, with overnight stays) if spouses are invited. In addition, spouses endure a lot while their partners are engaged in board work. Extending an invitation to the retreat is a way of expressing appreciation. If spouses attend, schedule activities for them during board sessions. Usually, spouses are invited to all receptions and meals, and sometimes to general sessions if the speaker and topic are of common interest.

Whether the invitation should extend only to spouses or also include guests is again a board decision. Today, with fewer "traditional" families, many boards leave it up to individual members whether to bring a guest. The category of retreat "guest" may include people with various ties to individual board members or the organization.

The question of who pays for spouses or guests should be determined early in the planning process. Often, organizations pay for guests' room and meals, and sometimes for travel.

■ **The media and general public.** Boards that are subject to open-meeting laws face a special challenge: The presence of the news media or the public may inhibit open and frank board discussions. Check with legal counsel about what kinds of meetings could be exempt from open meeting laws. Often, by its nature, a board retreat sounds dull to reporters, and they may opt not to cover it.

■ **Honorary and emeritus trustees.** Usually, retreats are intended for the "working board." However, if honorary or emeritus trustees remain involved in board activities, the retreat planning committee can consider inviting them to attend.

## Orienting New Board Members

A retreat can be a wonderful opportunity to bring new board members fully into the fold — or alienate them forever. We all know what it's like to be the new person in a group of old friends who know how things are done. Don't simply assume that new board members will understand the pace and culture of your board's retreats.

Experienced retreat facilitator Linda Moore suggests creating a mechanism for welcoming new members and informing them about what to expect — what to wear; whether the group stays up late into the night or goes to bed early to be fresh for sessions at 7:00 a.m.; if the group works nonstop or takes long breaks at midday for walks in the country; how to find partners for tennis or golf.

## Effectively Incorporating Speakers

Good speakers stimulate thinking by bringing fresh expertise, insight, and information to the board. Speakers may come from inside or outside the organization. The key to using speakers effectively is to ensure that they don't dominate the retreat. The agenda should incorporate opportunities for question-and-answer sessions and board problem-solving and team-building exercises. Speakers are useful in raising issues and providing shortcuts to the heart of issues. They should not be brought in to present solutions or formulas for the board to follow in working toward the retreat's objectives.

# WHEN & WHERE?

To be successful, a retreat needs to be timed appropriately. It isn't a good idea to expect board members to focus on a retreat when other pressing matters are at hand that can't be solved by a retreat. And as we noted in the "Why?" chapter, a retreat won't be effective if the board hasn't really thought out what it hopes to accomplish through the retreat. A retreat that's undertaken just for the sake of having a retreat is not only going to be ineffective, it's going to negatively affect members' attitudes toward future retreats.

So, in scheduling a retreat, it's important to build in time for planning. Remember, the retreat planning committee has to solicit input from all board members, engage the right facilitator and speakers, plan and refine the agenda, develop an invitation list and send out invitations with sufficient advance notice, select the right site, and attend to all the details that make any complex meeting a success. Some boards plan their retreat dates a year in advance, while others find that three to six months is enough time for members to commit to specific dates.

## Setting the Date

In selecting a retreat date, ask board members and other participants for input on the best days of the week, desired locations, and start/end times. Ask those polled to think about all of the other conflicts that may occur — family responsibilities, work schedule conflicts, even major sporting events. No board retreat can be counted a success unless it has at least 80 percent attendance, and the aim should be for 100 percent.

## Mapping Out the Schedule

One-and-a-half to two days is about the time needed for a focused, in-depth board retreat. An overnight stay presents opportunities for informal socialization and relationship-building that can't be orchestrated in the context of formal meetings and discussions. Few board members will be willing to participate in a retreat that drags on for longer than three days. Remember, a retreat should focus on one or two issues at most. Don't try to squeeze in too much.

## Getting Away From It All

A retreat should be held in an environment conducive to accomplishing the goals you set for it — but it is very important to be far enough away to keep participants focused on the work at hand and eliminate the temptation to go back to the office.

Of course, you can do your best to take board members away from daily work and family responsibilities, but in an age of cell phones, beepers, and e-mail, it can be helpful to remind board members that the retreat requires their complete attention and focus. A facilitator can be helpful in laying the ground rules: No telephones (wire or wireless), beepers, or e-mail in the meeting area, and no sneaking away during sessions to reconnect with the outside world.

Choose your location so that it is accessible given the restrictions of budget and time available, but at least an hour away from the area where most board members live and work. The retreat location should provide opportunities for recreation as well as work. Even if relationship-building isn't a major agenda item, it should be an auxiliary benefit of a board retreat. Opportunities to play together can forge meaningful bonds, helping board members discover common ground that they will be able to access back in the board room.

In addition, the retreat site should provide facilities appropriate for the retreat activities planned. For example, if the board retreat's goal is to develop a technology master plan for the organization, then you might choose a meeting location that will let board members have hands-on access to some of the hardware and software being considered. If the retreat goal is to build trust and cohesiveness, then the meeting might best be set in an environment that allows board members to work together to achieve a common goal — teaming up to cook meals, for example, or to build a Habitat for Humanity house or complete an Outward Bound–style wilderness or "ropes" course.

Other things to look for in a retreat facility include:

- Comfortable meeting rooms (the ability to control the rooms' temperature is a plus), including small rooms for breakout sessions.

- Good audiovisual capabilities and support services.

- Appropriate accommodations and food services.

- Affordability.

- Hospitality.

- Attentive conference staff.

- Attractive grounds and recre-

# On the Road

When planning your next board retreat, consider taking the board on the road. Here's how three organizations put a new spin on board retreats.

## On the Bus

The board of a foundation held a retreat while riding on a bus to visit some of the organizations they had been funding. Board members, usually dressed in business attire, were asked to don jeans and hard hats while getting a firsthand view of the programs and facilities with which they had been associated but had never seen. In between their visits and a box lunch, the facilitator led the group discussions. By bringing the board closer to the mission of the organization, on the second day of the retreat, board members were able to make stronger decisions about the future direction of the foundation.·

## On the Water

An association board facing some challenging decisions for the future of their organization held their once-a-year retreat aboard a cruise ship. Using the ship's executive conference room for meetings, work was done while at sea and additional group time was planned while at port and at meals. Because the issues that the board was discussing at this retreat were of critical importance, the retreat planners were sure to schedule time for varying group activities on the ship. The results of the retreat were positive for everyone, including the organization.

## On the Train

The board of a performing arts organization got their meeting on track by conducting their retreat on a train. During the one-and-a half day trip, meetings took place in a train car designed especially for this 12-member board, and the group gathered for meals in the train's dining car. When the train stopped at its midpoint destination, the board took a break for a guided tour of the city. Upon reboarding the train, they reconvened their meeting and finished their agenda by the time they reached their original departure station.

ational opportunities — especially golf, tennis, and hiking —for free time.

## Escaping the Boardroom: Alternative Meeting Spaces

The choice of a retreat location is often driven by such factors as budget and group size. At first glance, the board chair's dining room table may seem the perfect retreat locale; however, if your goal is full attendance, you'll have a better chance of achieving this if the retreat is planned for a location that offers not only appropriate meeting spaces, but also opportunities for social activities and recreation. A factor such as whether the retreat facility allows alcohol consumption may also be a prime consideration. Consider:

■ **Country inns and resorts.** Some country resorts promote themselves as retreat centers — complete with meeting rooms and a range of outdoor team-building activities. Bed-and-breakfast style inns can often be

reserved exclusively for a meeting, offering many opportunities for formal and informal gatherings.

■ **Campgrounds and lodges at state or national parks.** While sometimes rustic, the park systems offer a variety of accommodations in beautiful settings at a reasonable price — the most rustic can be perfect for groups with an interest in the outdoors or when Outward Bound–style adventures are planned. Early reservations (often a year in advance) may be required.

■ **Spiritual retreat centers.** Board members with religious affiliations may already have connections with such resources.

■ **University conference centers.** Both public and private institutions often offer meeting facilities. Some institutions have formal, well-appointed conference centers at rates similar to major hotels; others offer dorms and academic facilities in the summer and over winter breaks.

■ **Rental homes in the mountains, in the country, or at the beach.** A single home in a desirable location — or a group of homes close together — can accommodate different sized groups. Sharing living space, as well as

shopping and meal preparation responsibilities, isn't for everyone, but it can offer a rare opportunity for groups to cement their commitment to a common goal and discover one another's unique skills and perspectives.

■ **Corporate boardrooms and retreat centers.** Corporate supporters and board members who are corporate executives are probably familiar with a variety of meeting facilities and may be able to help the organization negotiate favorable costs — or even to underwrite some or all of the costs.

The most memorable and meaningful retreats tend to be built around a single, clearly defined theme. These retreats focus on one or two issues that are important to the board, and every participant clearly understands the retreat's objectives. Once it is clear what the board hopes to accomplish from the retreat, then the task is to determine what activities will best allow it to accomplish those objectives. Often, the task of planning an agenda is assigned to an experienced outside facilitator, who may work closely with the retreat planning committee, the chief executive, the board chair, or a combination of these three.

## Researching Information Important to the Retreat

The retreat is not the time or place for lengthy informational reports, and on some occasions, not much pre-retreat information, but board members should be well informed about the issues to be addressed at the retreat *before* they arrive. Although opinion and anecdotes can be very valuable, having an objective assessment can provide good data to work with.

- Some advance data-gathering will assist the facilitator and retreat planning committee in designing retreat goals, objectives, and agenda (see the pre-retreat questionnaire samples on page 9–11).

- Environmental data on trends and new developments that could affect the organization's future and organizational data on key performance indicators (finances, service volume, program growth, human resources) should be disseminated in advance of the retreat to all participants.

- Perception and market data gathered through pre-retreat surveys of the board, executive management, professional staff, or the community at large may be presented at the retreat, where they can be explained and discussed at length.

- Articles and background material can inspire thinking and new approaches to your issues.

The types and amount of data gathered and disseminated will, of course, depend on the focus of the retreat.

- *A strategic planning retreat*, for example, will generally require information that offers perspective on trends and factors affecting the organization's ability to achieve its mission now and in the future — financial trends, demographic changes, new technology or research findings, competition, and legislative and regulatory trends.

- *Board development and leadership relationship retreats* can benefit from confidential pre-retreat questionnaires or interviews focusing on issues that board members may be reluctant to discuss openly, such as problems in the board–executive relationship or the role of the board chair. A skilled facilitator can use questionnaire results to intro-

*The importance of the getting-to-know-one-another piece of a retreat shouldn't be underestimated. It's the place where board members reestablish their common goals and recognize that they share common values. This isn't something that happens in the day-to-day work of the board because boards are very task-oriented. The executive and the nominating committee may be the only ones who truly understand why all of these people were brought together. Board members need opportunities to get to know one another so they can feel comfortable working together for a common goal.*

— Linda Moore
President
Community Solutions
International
Washington, DC

duce such issues in a non-threatening manner. Both questionnaires and one-on-one interviews are best administered by an objective outsider, such as the retreat facilitator. To ensure confidentiality, questionnaires should be returned directly to the facilitator and not processed by the retreat planning committee or executive office. The facilitator will prepare results to share with the board. If the planning committee or executive tallies questionnaire results, then anonymity can be preserved by providing all board members with identical, postage-paid return envelopes and asking them not to write their names on the questionnaires.

## Paving the Way for Full Participation

Before the meeting, all participants should receive a package including the meeting agenda and reading materials. Usually, the executive staff, in accordance with the direction of the retreat planning committee, will handle information dissemination. Invitees will be asked to R.S.V.P. promptly, and, if necessary, executive staff will follow up with nonrespondents. If key players don't respond or plan not

to attend, an appropriate, influential leader (board chair, retreat planning chair, or executive) can contact these individuals and explain why their participation is important. The goal is 100 percent participation. Full participation is only possible when board leaders prove that they believe the retreat is important. Discourage board members from arriving late or leaving early. Late arrivals can be disruptive to the proceedings when participants need to be brought up to speed, and those with early departures may miss out in contributing critical information to important discussions.

## Breaking the Ice

People work best in groups when they are relaxed and comfortable with one another. Humor and joy incorporated in ice-breakers are a powerful force in "jelling" a group. The ice-breaker could be a social event that precedes each formal session or a group exercise that starts the meeting. When boards charter a bus or other transportation to a retreat, the trip itself can act as an ice-breaker. Ways to break the ice at the start of a meeting are as varied as the organizations we serve. In selecting an ice-breaker, consider the culture and style of your organization. The ice-breaker could consist of simply asking board members to stand up, introduce themselves, and perhaps share something about themselves, such as a favorite movie or hobby;

or the exercise could be a little more elaborate, requiring some advanced planning. Some suggestions:

- **Baby Pictures** — A few days before the retreat, ask participants to provide the facilitator with photos of themselves as children. Over a morning coffee break or after a lunch hour, the facilitator posts the photos, and participants match photos with board members. The facilitator can be responsible for providing the paper and pencils.

- **Treasure Hunt** — Before the retreat, the facilitator should find out two or three facts about each participant that no one else in the group knows. At the retreat, give each participant a copy of the list and ask them to match each person with their facts.

- **Who Am I?** — Make a list of different couples from history, entertainment, politics, etc. (Bonnie and Clyde, Marc Antony and Cleopatra, Bob Hope and Bing Crosby). Write each name on a pressure-sensitive label and randomly affix the labels to members backs as they arrive, making sure the members don't see the name they receive. Their job is to guess who they are by asking other members questions like, "Am I a historical figure?

Am I alive today? Am I male or female?" Once they determine who their character is, they need to find their partner.

- **"Sole" Mates** — Ask the members of the group to find people in the room who share their birthday month, alma mater, number of children, favorite pro football team, shoe size, etc.

- **Ace Reporter** — Have participants choose someone in the room they don't know well and interview him or her; take turns around the room introducing this person to the group.

- **Match That Tune** — On a table as participants arrive are pieces of paper bearing the first lines of songs from the '20s through the '90s. Members of different generations team up to match the first lines with the names of the songs.

## Gaining Buy-in

Once the ice has been broken and members are ready to get down to work, it's helpful to take a moment to reconfirm the retreat's objectives and agenda. The facilitator describes the retreat's goals, objectives, and agenda, and then asks the group, "Does everyone agree with these objectives?" and "Should anything else be on the agenda?" If the retreat planning has been done well and is based on data from thoughtful pre-

retreat research, then the entire board should quickly indicate their buy-in to the process.

If members raise objections or suggest additional agenda items, then a skilled facilitator will be able to incorporate pertinent and achievable agenda items or list them on a flip chart labeled "items for the future." By listening to any ensuing discussions, a good facilitator will also be able to identify participants who may have a tendency to crusade, monopolize, or otherwise disrupt the flow of the meeting, so that he or she can deal diplomatically with them throughout the process.

Beginning the meeting with an inclusive buy-in discussion signals to participants that the purpose of the meeting is open, not hidden. Members recognize that the democratic process is at work, everyone's views will be heard, and the facilitator is there to channel the meeting to a productive conclusion. The facilitator should also stress that some basic courtesies must be followed while in the meeting. Side conversations and interruptions should be discouraged while others are speaking, and the meeting's confidentiality should be respected.

## An Exercise in Reality

Most board members believe that their activities for the organization are geared towards the institution's greatest needs. Bill Dietel, chair of the Pierson-Lovelace Foundation, recalls a retreat exercise that helped board members see how far they sometimes stray from priorities in managing their board service time.

1. For a month before the retreat, have board members log all of the time they put into board work onto their calendars. Have them copy that month's calendar and bring it to the retreat.

2. Early in the retreat, have board members brainstorm about the board activities that are most vital to helping the institution thrive — narrow this list to a set of board service priorities and estimate what percentage of his or her time each board member should devote to each activity.

**And/or...**

2. Without the benefit of their calendars, have board members estimate what percentage of their board service time is devoted to each activity they do for the organization — fund-raising, committee work, financial oversight, etc.

3. Have them compare these estimates and the real percentage of time spent on different activities as revealed by their monthly logs.

Use the mismatch between priorities and actual activities to discuss how board members can better serve the organization and how the organization can better use board members' time.

## Getting to Work

Each retreat will include content that's specifically tailored to meet the objectives set by the board. If the retreat is a strategic-planning exercise, then it may have a cyclical format — beginning with full-group briefings on key issues, branching out into breakout planning sessions, and returning for full-group negotiation of implementation items. If the retreat's purpose is primarily to encourage better relationships, then it may take a much more informal approach. In fact, participants in such retreats may never enter a meeting room, but may dive right into hands-on projects that encourage members to get to know one another and use skills not normally put to work in the boardroom.

Some retreats will include one or more speakers, but it's best to keep formal speeches and long informational presentations to a minimum. A good practice is that every board member present at the retreat should speak during the first 30 minutes of the retreat — even if it's just to say his or her name. And there should be many opportunities for each voice to be heard throughout the retreat. It is the role of the facilitator, along with an attentive board chair, to see that this is accomplished.

Another trap is to overschedule the retreat out of fear that participants will get bored. Allow as much opportunity as possible for discussion, and structure the agenda with enough flexibility to encourage participation and allow the group to explore an interesting line of thought. A good facilitator will ensure that the group gets back on track in plenty of time to achieve its objectives. Avoid having too many handouts. Make effective use of flip charts, overheads, videos, and Microsoft PowerPoint presentations.

Small discussion groups and case exercises encourage full participation. An ideal discussion group will number six to nine participants — big enough for diversity but small enough so everyone has a chance to participate. If a retreat is larger than about 15 members, consider dividing into smaller groups when it's time for brainstorming or developing action ideas. Give the groups a specific task (for example, "Which board committees can we eliminate?") and a time limit. Usually, the less time given, the better. Provide groups with flip charts and pens for recording their ideas to share with the larger group. Then, reconvene the entire board, have each group report, and summarize the recommenda-

tions on a flip chart. After each small group reports, open the topic for general discussion and aim at, if possible, consensus.

At various times throughout the retreat, the facilitator should "check in" with the attendees to gain their agreement with the progress toward its retreat goals.

## Taking Breaks

The retreat agenda should allow time for members to talk informally and relax. During long sessions, some facilitators will bring in an aerobics instructor to get the group moving at whatever pace suits each participant. There should be plenty of breaks for snacks and beverages, and regular meal breaks.

Food can have an important impact on group dynamics. Plan for a light lunch that does not include pasta. Serving pasta for lunch will make participants sleepy. Also, avoid serving alcohol during meeting times. Make sure there is plenty of water and mints or candy available on the tables throughout the retreat; a mid-afternoon coffee break with cookies, brownies, or fruit will help to keep participants awake.

## Closing the Meeting

If the retreat is designed to generate specific actions or decisions, the facilitator may help the group to summarize an action plan to expedite follow-up. A good action plan clearly states what will be done, who has responsibility for follow-up, and when results are expected.

The board chair usually has the last word, thanking the board for its participation and reaffirming his or her initial commitment to the retreat process. The retreat should end on a high note. Even if the goal was not to develop a list of specific actions, the facilitator, chair, or chief executive should take a moment at the end to summarize what has been accomplished.

# Find Your Seat: Room Arrangements That Work

Seating arrangements can have a tremendous effect on session interactions and group dynamics. Here are some guidelines.

## Do Consider:

■ **An informal circle.** Comfortable couches and chairs arranged in a circle — facilitates full participation and eliminates hierarchies. Accommodates 15-20 people.

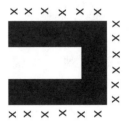

■ **U-shape.** Tables and chairs arranged along three sides, with one end open for presenters — ensures that everyone can see and hear presentations and, as with a circle, encourages participation. Appropriate for groups of no more than 25.

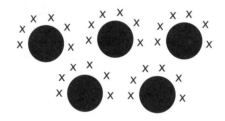

■ **Rounds of 6.** Six chairs at a series of round tables, arranged so that no backs face the front of the room — appropriate for full participation and small group break-out sessions. Can accommodate any size group; best for larger groups.

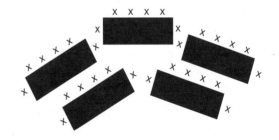

■ **Clusters of rectangles.** Six to eight people at a series of rectangular tables arranged at an angle (a variation on the theme of rounds). Good for small group break out sessions — usually used if no round tables are available. Can accommodate any size group; best for larger groups.

■ **Single tables.** Tables angled with a single central aisle in the center — allows participants to see one another while still facing the front of the room. Can accommodate any size group; best for larger groups.

## Don't Even Think About:

*Theater or classroom style.* Both arrangements discourage participation and open discussion because the central focus is the speaker. These arrangements are hierarchical rather than democratic. They foster passive absorption of information (and the accompanying boredom), not the sorts of strategic conversations and brainstorming that comprise an effective retreat. Disadvantages include:

- Impossible for all participants to see one another.

- Difficult to break out into small groups.

- Possible for individuals to hide — or even to doze through sessions.

- Small classroom desks and theater seats without tables make it difficult for participants to take notes, manage resource materials gracefully, and enjoy refreshments.

- Narrow aisles discourage participants from standing and stretching periodically.

# Don't Forget to Pack Your Sense of Humor

Have you heard the one about the three board members? Probably not. Serving as a member of a nonprofit board is no joke, but it should be a laughing matter, according to psychologists, who stress the importance of having a good laugh now and then — in the boardroom, and especially at a board retreat.

While boards may be addressing serious organizational challenges in a retreat setting, there can be proper uses of boardroom humor to accomplish and even facilitate the critical work of the board and individual board members — even in some of the most difficult times.

Included in the skills that a facilitator brings to the retreat process should be a sense of humor, along with the knowledge of how and when to use it to the group's full benefit.

Humor can be used to defuse tense situations and conflict. With an appropriate witty remark, followed by a burst of laughter, the air is cleared and all can refocus on the task at hand. A second use is to create rapport and solicit feedback — among board members and between the board and the chief executive. This can be accomplished with an ice-breaker exercise, by scheduling in fun group activities, or through some self-deprecating humor from the chair of the board.

Another use for humor is to make difficult messages more agreeable to fellow board members, like softening the blow that a grant you were expecting did not materialize. This says to the board, we're all in this together. Humor allows us to stand back and see an issue from a different perspective.

Consider including cartoons in the retreat handbook or slipping a humorous image into an overhead presentation. Like the good work of the board itself, effective humor lies in good timing, unpredictability, positiveness, and conciseness.

# WHAT NEXT?

As a general rule, boards take no votes and make no official decisions at a retreat. The retreat format is designed to encourage full participation and creative thinking. The retreat atmosphere is compromised if someone calls for an "executive" or closed session at a retreat. A retreat is not the place to hold such a session, especially since retreat participants (including special guests, staff, etc.) were decided upon in the planning phase. Voting detracts from this open, participative, relaxed atmosphere. Formal votes should be left for subsequent business meetings. The post-retreat interval can be used for staff or committees to clean up loose ends. Many a mission statement that looked brilliant on a flip chart at the end of a long, hard retreat sounds a little less clear the next day. Before the board votes, the executive or chairperson can make modest edits in the words while retaining the meaning. A post-retreat evaluation questionnaire may be sent to participants for assessing results and planning the next retreat.

## Sample Action Plan 1 – Strategic Planning Retreat

| Action | Who Expedites | By When |
|---|---|---|
| *Mission Statement:* The mission was generally reaffirmed as being an accurate, current statement of our reason for being. Wording changes were suggested. | Planning Committee and management to revise and submit to the board. | Next board meeting. |
| *Strategic Plan:* Broaden strategic plan to reflect longer-term (3–5 years) vision and its major strategic goals. Continue evolution of strategic-planning process as a tool for board-management communication, priority setting, and decision making. | Planning Committee. | Draft ready for year-end review. |

## Sample Action Plan 2 – Board Development Retreat

| Action | Who Expedites | By When |
|---|---|---|
| *Board Meetings:* Focus board time more on issues, not maintenance (e.g., finance reports). Reduce "canned" present-ation time. Use board calendar to schedule policy issues for discussion. | Board chairperson/ chief executive. | Calendar in place by January. |
| *Conflict Management:* Make board aware of potential opposition and conflicts when it reviews major proposals and inform board if conflicts have or can be resolved. | Board chairperson/ chief executive. | Ongoing. |

■ *Don't plan a retreat without the full commitment of board and executive leadership.* Board members will take their cue about what is important from the board chair and chief executive. Both must indicate early in the process that they believe the retreat is an important enterprise. Without the commitment of leadership it will be difficult to get full attendance, and near-perfect attendance is essential for retreat success.

■ *Don't hold a retreat without taking the time first to establish realistic, meaningful objectives.* Regular, ongoing retreats can be an invaluable tool for board development and for addressing important issues. They are also a costly investment — in the board's time and the organization's resources. Experience with poorly planned or ineffective retreats can undermine the board's willingness to commit to future retreats. Also, clear objectives are important for assessing the effectiveness of the retreat.

■ *Don't base retreat objectives on the opinions or ideas of one person or a small group of board leaders.* Retreat planning should be an inclusive, democratic process. All board members should feel that their input was valued by the retreat planning committee.

■ *Don't site your retreat too close to home and work.* To truly focus on the hands-on work of a retreat, participants must be able to separate themselves from their day-to-day work. Retreats should be held at a distance from the place where most board members live and work. Telephones, beepers, and e-mail should be banned from meeting rooms.

■ *Don't give participants too much pre-retreat homework.* Provide the information they will need to be full participants in the retreat process, but don't load them down with paper.

■ *Don't wait until the last minute to get your facilitator involved.* If you are using an outside facilitator, make sure you take the time to bring that person up to speed early in the planning process. A good facilitator can be an invaluable resource in retreat planning, and the more he or she knows about your organization and board, the more effectively the facilitator can help you achieve your retreat objectives. Evaluate facilitator and speakers in advance. Check references and, if possible, meet with speakers and facilitator before engaging them.

■ *Don't adhere to a "business-as-usual" format.* Using an outside facilitator and getting away from the usual business meeting site can help break patterns and encourage full participation. Don't let the same people dominate discussions. Don't let the retreat be taken up by long informational presentations or normal board business.

■ *Don't schedule a rigid, inflexible agenda.* Leave room for discussion and exploration. A good meeting agenda is both focused *and* flexible.

■ *Don't forget fun.* Even if the purpose of the board retreat isn't to build better board relationships, this should be an important side benefit of the retreat. Remember that a retreat is a joyful, human, and humane activity, and informal interactions among board members should be encouraged.

# Do!

This board retreat checklist covers the full range of tasks required to plan and conduct a successful *forward retreat*.

| Action Item | Assigned To | Date Due |
|---|---|---|
| ***Commitment by Leadership and Membership*** | | |
| ❑ Board chairperson endorses retreat | _____ | _____ |
| ❑ Chief executive commits to involvement | _____ | _____ |
| ❑ Appoint planning task force | _____ | _____ |
| ***Objective Setting*** | | |
| ❑ Develop pre-retreat board questionnaire | _____ | _____ |
| ❑ Mail pre-retreat questionnaire | _____ | _____ |
| ❑ Distribute and gather results of questionnaire | _____ | _____ |
| ❑ Interview key board members | _____ | _____ |
| ❑ Planning committee meets to determine issues for retreat | _____ | _____ |
| ❑ Adopt overall purpose and specific objectives based on questionnaire or other diagnostic tool | _____ | _____ |
| ❑ Objectives are clear and realistic | | |
| ❑ Communicate objectives with full board | | |
| ❑ Full board endorses objectives | _____ | _____ |
| ***Planning and Preparation*** | | |
| ❑ Choose facilitator and negotiate terms | _____ | _____ |
| ❑ Engage facilitator (signed contract specifying terms) | _____ | _____ |
| ❑ Facilitator confers in person or over the phone with planning committee to prepare agenda and discuss logistics | _____ | _____ |
| ❑ Develop invitation list including: | | |
| • Current board members and executive | _____ | _____ |
| • Honorary/emeritus board members? | _____ | _____ |
| • Non-board committee members? | _____ | _____ |

| Action Item | Assigned To | Date Due |
|---|---|---|
| •   Spouses and guests? | _____ | _____ |
| •   Senior management? | _____ | _____ |
| •   Professional staff? | _____ | _____ |
| •   Others | _____ | _____ |
| •   Others | _____ | _____ |
| •   Others | _____ | _____ |
| •   Others | _____ | _____ |
| ❑  Select date and length of retreat | _____ | _____ |
| ❑  Select speakers (if desired) and negotiate terms | _____ | _____ |
| ❑  Engage speakers (signed contract specifying terms) | _____ | _____ |
| ❑  Draft agenda submitted and approved | _____ | _____ |
| Choose retreat site; special considerations include: | | |
| •   Distance | _____ | _____ |
| •   Meeting facilities | _____ | _____ |
| •   Recreational opportunities | _____ | _____ |
| •   Cost | _____ | _____ |
| •   Other issues | _____ | _____ |
| •   Other issues | _____ | _____ |
| •   Other issues | _____ | _____ |
| •   Other issues | _____ | _____ |
| ❑  Logistical details verified, including: | | |
| •   Travel arrangements | _____ | _____ |
| •   Lodging arrangements and checkout times | _____ | _____ |
| •   Programming for spouses and guests | _____ | _____ |
| •   Reception and meal arrangements | _____ | _____ |
| •   Audiovisual equipment (projectors, flipcharts) | _____ | _____ |
| •   Participant materials packet preparation | _____ | _____ |
| •   Participant materials packet delivery | _____ | _____ |
| •   Others | _____ | _____ |
| •   Others | _____ | _____ |
| ❑  Prepare background information for retreat | _____ | _____ |

| Action Item | Assigned To | Date Due |
|---|---|---|
| *Meeting Dynamics* | | |
| ❑ Finalize agenda that addresses meeting objectives | _____ | _____ |
| ❑ Review agenda to ensure it balances presentations with board activity | _____ | _____ |
| ❑ Plan time for work, socializing, recreation, and free time | _____ | _____ |
| *Follow-up Actions* | | |
| ❑ Prepare action plan | _____ | _____ |
| ❑ Distribute plan to all participants | _____ | _____ |
| ❑ Disseminate and tally retreat evaluation survey | _____ | _____ |
| ❑ Gather responses and commitments for action | _____ | _____ |
| ❑ Follow up on plan progress | _____ | _____ |
| ❑ Schedule next retreat | _____ | _____ |

# Retreat Planning Process

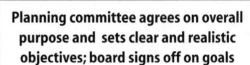

**Commitment by board leadership, chief executive, and all board members**

**Board follows up on retreat action plan**

**Planning committee agrees on overall purpose and sets clear and realistic objectives; board signs off on goals**

**At retreat, participants accomplish objectives and develop post-retreat action plan**

**Planning committee selects and contracts with skilled, experienced facilitator**

**Pertinent data gathered by board and staff**

**Planning committee prepares draft agenda and determines location and schedule**

# Suggested Resources

Andringa, Robert C. and Ted W. Engstrom. *Nonprofit Board Answer Book: Practical Guidelines for Board Members and Chief Executives.* Washington, DC: BoardSource, 2001, 300 pages.

BoardSource has created the next best thing to sitting down face to face with thousands of board members and chief executives! Our new expanded edition of the best-selling *Nonprofit Board Answer Book* is organized in an easy-to-follow question and answer format and covers almost every situation you're likely to encounter in nonprofit board governance. Building on the phenomenal success of the first edition, this new expanded edition includes 25 brand new chapters offering comprehensive coverage of the nuts and bolts you need to build a quality board.

BoardSource and Kathleen Fletcher. *The Policy Sampler: A Resource for Nonprofit Boards.* Washington, DC: BoardSource, 2000, 52 pages, plus diskette.

In addition to steering the nonprofit organization's activities, nonprofit boards are also responsible for setting policies that govern their own actions. This new resource from BoardSource provides nonprofit leaders with more than 70 sample board policies and job descriptions collected from a wide variety of nonprofits. The user's guide provides a basic overview for each of the policies. The diskette contains the full selection of sample policies and job descriptions that can be easily customized to suit your organization.

Jones, Ken. *Icebreakers: A Sourcebook of Games, Exercises and Simulations.* San Diego, CA: Pfeiffer & Company, 1991, 237 pages.

This resource provides hundreds of ice-breaking exercises and simulations for any size group. Also includes photo-ready participant and facilitator worksheets.

BoardSource. *Blueprint for Success: A Guide to Strategic Planning for Nonprofit Board Members.* (Video) Washington, DC: BoardSource, 1997, 25 minutes, plus 20-page user's guide.

In this video production, NBC News broadcast journalist Maria Shriver, a board member of Special Olympics International, guides an exploration of how two nonprofit organizations carry out strategic planning. The video is the perfect motivational tool for nonprofit boards considering a strategic plan, for board members who are unfamiliar with strategic planning, or as inspiration for boards about to embark on the process. The free user's guide includes guidelines and discussion questions that allow a board to use the video as a training tool, a starting point for in-depth discussion on strategic planning.

Hughes, Sandra R., Berit M. Lakey, and Marla J. Bobowick. *The Board Building Cycle: Nine Steps to Finding, Recruiting, and Engaging Nonprofit Board Members.* Washington, DC: BoardSource, 2000, 52 pages, plus diskette.

*The Board Building Cycle* features nine-steps for your board to follow through the board development process, providing helpful tips on what motivates people to join boards, how and where to find board members, ideas for conducting an orientation session, and specific tasks for the board's governance committee. Included are suggestions for involving former board members as advisors or committee members and removing difficult or ineffective board members.

BoardSource. *Meeting the Challenge: An Orientation to Nonprofit Board Service.* (Video) Washington, DC: BoardSource, 1998, 45 minutes, plus a 20-page user's guide.

Hosted by Ray Suarez, voice of National Public Radio's *Talk of the Nation,* highlights four basic principles of board responsibility — determining mission and program, ensuring effective oversight, providing resources, and participating in community outreach. The video features interviews with board members, executive directors, and experts in the field of board governance as they share their experiences and insights into nonprofit board service. Ideal for use as a board orientation tool and as a starting point for board development and strategic planning. The video is equally suited for viewing at home by an individual board member or as a group activity.

BoardSource. *Speaking of Money: A Guide to Fundraising for Non-profit Board Members.* (Video) Washington, DC: BoardSource, 1996, 30 minutes, plus 20-page user's guide.

Fund-raising is one of the most challenging and critical areas of board responsibility. In this video, real board members from a variety of organizations discuss fund-raising basics, successes, and critical considerations. Issues discussed include fund-raising as a basic responsibility, working in partner-ship with the staff, creating a strong case, stages of the development process, personal contributions, skill of asking for a gift. This video is equally suitable at a board orientation session, development committee meeting, or board retreat. Its user's guide, written by consultant Kay Sprinkel Grace, provides an excellent reinforce-ment for discussion.

BoardSource. *The Board Meeting Rescue Kit: 20 Ideas for Jumpstarting Your Board Meetings.* Washington, DC: BoardSource, 2001, 27 pages.

Increase the productivity and efficiency of your board meetings. The ideas in this booklet will inspire your board on new ways to liven up discussions, streamline board procedures, increase effectiveness, and save valuable time. Learn how to transform your board meetings into productive, efficient discussions that foster relevant, helpful contributions from all board members. Also included are sample board meeting agendas, board meeting evaluations, and sample board minutes.

BoardSource. *Self-Assessment for Nonprofit Governing Boards.* Washington, DC: BoardSource, revised 1999, user's guide 60 pages, individual board member ques-tionnaire 24 pages.

This kit, relying heavily on the BoardSource best-seller *Ten Basic Responsibilities of Nonprofit Boards,* helps board members analyze their own strengths and weaknesses and assess the overall performance of the board. The assessment kit includes 15 ques-tionnaires to be distributed to individual board members (addi-tional booklets available in sets of five) and a user's guide to help with the interpretation of the data, as well as setting up a constructive meeting to discuss the results afterwards with the full board. *Self-Assessment* is an ideal prepara-tion for a board retreat or an annual performance review. It is also a valuable tool for consultants and facilitators.

# About the Author

*Dr. Sandra R. Hughes* currently serves as Executive Consultant of BoardSource. In addition to having served as a consultant and facilitator for the past eight years, she has held various management positions at the United States Rowing Association, American Bar Association, George Williams College, Levi Strauss & Company, the Levi Strauss Foundation, the University of Tennessee, and *The Christian Science Monitor.*

Hughes received her bachelor of arts degree in English from the University of Maryland and also holds a masters degree in counseling and a doctorate in administration and organizational behavior. She has special interests in and has presented numerous seminars and workshops, and written articles on the psychology of humor; the philosophy of management and organizational behavior; fundraising and resource development;

and the psychology of sport. She also facilitates and leads programs in strategic thinking and planning, board training and leadership, resource development, fundraising, sponsorship, membership services and marketing, organization culture and values, management training, change, teamwork, effective meetings, and human resource training.

## The BoardSource Council of Editorial Advisors

Robert Andringa, President, Coalition for Christian Colleges and Universities

Randy Blackmon, Assistant Director of Research, Indiana University

Peter Berns, Executive Director, Maryland Association of Nonprofits

Russell Cargo, Director, George Mason University Department of Nonprofit Management

Bruce Collins, Vice President and General Counsel, C-SPAN

Ann Dalton, Managing Director, Association of Junior Leagues International

Melissa Davis, Associate Director, YMCA of the USA

Michael Glomb, Attorney, Feldsman, Tucker, Leifer, Fidell & Bank

Ellen Hirzy, writer, editor

Thomas P. Holland, Professor, University of Georgia School of Social Work

Ann Hoover, Executive Director, Community Partnership with Youth

Bruce Hopkins, Attorney, Polsinelli, White, Vardman & Sha

Irv Katz, Group Vice President, Community Impact, United Way of America

Daniel Kemp, Trustee/Volunteer Resource Center Manager, Opera America

Ann Kent, Manager, Services to Nonprofits, Business Volunteer Center

Daniel Kurtz, Attorney, Gilbert, Segall, & Young

David LaPiana, President, LaPiana Associates

Mark Light, President, First Light

Brooke Mahoney, Executive Director, Volunteer Consulting Group, Inc.

Jan Masaoka, Executive Director, Support Center for Nonprofit Management

Kumi Naidoo, Secretary-General/CEO, CIVICUS

Paul Pritchard, President, National Park Trust

Cinthia Schuman, Associate Director, Nonprofit Sector Research Fund

# Have You Used These BoardSource Resources?

## Videos

*Meeting the Challenge: An Orientation to Nonprofit Board Service*

*Blueprint for Success: A Guide to Strategic Planning for Nonprofit Board Members*

*Speaking of Money: A Guide to Fund-Raising for Nonprofit Board Members*

*Building A Successful Team: A Nonprofit's Guide to Board Development*

## Books

*The Board Development Planner: A Calendar of Nonprofit Board Initiatives*

*The Board Chair Handbook*

*Managing Conflicts of Interest: Practical Guidelines for Nonprofit Boards*

*Checks and Balances: The Board Member's Guide to Nonprofit Financial Audits*

*The Board-Savvy CEO: How To Build a Strong, Positive Relationship with Your Board*

*Presenting: Board Orientation*

*Presenting: Nonprofit Financials*

*The Board Meeting Rescue Kit: 20 Ideas for Jumpstarting Your Board Meetings*

*Nonprofit Governance: Steering Your Organization with Authority and Accountability*

*The Board Building Cycle: Nine Steps to Finding, Recruiting, and Engaging Nonprofit Board Members*

*The Policy Sampler: A Resource for Nonprofit Boards*

*Chief Executive Compensation*

*To Go Forward, Retreat! The Board Retreat Handbook*

*Turning Vision into Reality: What the Founding Board Should Know about Starting a Nonprofit Organization*

*Nonprofit Board Answer Book*

*Leaving Nothing to Chance: Achieving Board Accountability through Risk Management*

*The Legal Obligations of Nonprofit Boards*

*Self-Assessment for Nonprofit Governing Boards*

*Assessment of the Chief Executive*

*Fearless Fund-Raising*

*Hiring the Chief Executive: A Practical Guide to the Search and Selection Process*

*The Nonprofit Board's Guide to Bylaws*

*Creating and Using Investment Policies*

*Planned Giving*

*Capital Campaigns: Fund-Raising Guidelines for Board Members*

*Transforming Board Structure: New Possibilities for Committees and Task Forces*

*Preventing Fraud: How To Safeguard Your Organization*

## Governance Series

1. *Ten Basic Responsibilities of Nonprofit Boards (available on audiotape)*

2. *The Chief Executive's Role in Developing the Nonprofit Board*

3. *Creating Strong Board-Staff Partnerships*

4. *The Chair's Role in Leading the Nonprofit Board*

5. *How to Help Your Board Govern More and Manage Less (available on audiotape)*

6. *The Board's Role in Strategic Planning (available on audiotape)*

7. *Financial Responsibilities of the Nonprofit Board*

8. *Understanding Nonprofit Financial Statements*

9. *Fund-Raising and the Nonprofit Board Member (available on audiotape)*

10. *Evaluation and the Nonprofit Board*

*For an up-to-date list of publications and information about current prices, membership, and other services, please call BoardSource at 800-883-6262 or visit our bookstore at www.boardsource.org.*